THE LIVING FESTIVALS SERIES

Jack Priestley — Series Editor

Guru Nanak's Birthday

MARGARET DAVIDSON

RMEP

RELIGIOUS AND MORAL EDUCATION PRESS

An Imprint of Arnold-Wheaton

Religious and Moral Education Press
An Imprint of Arnold-Wheaton
Hennock Road, Exeter EX2 8RP

Pergamon Press Ltd
Headington Hill Hall, Oxford OX3 0BW

Pergamon Press Inc.
Maxwell House, Fairview Park, Elmsford, New York 10523

Pergamon Press Canada Ltd
Suite 104, 150 Consumers Road, Willowdale, Ontario M2J 1P9

Pergamon Press (Australia) Pty Ltd
P.O. Box 544, Potts Point, N.S.W. 2011

Pergamon Press GmbH
Hammerweg 6, D-6242 Kronberg, Federal Republic of Germany

First published 1982

Reprinted 1983

Printed in Great Britain by A. Wheaton & Co. Ltd, Exeter

ISBN 0 08-027877-9 non net
0 08-027878-7 net

ACKNOWLEDGEMENTS

The author and publisher wish to thank the following organizations
and individuals who kindly provided photographs: The British
Museum; Ann and Bury Peerless.

The author and series editor accept full responsibility for the
statements made in this book. They would, however, like to place on
record their appreciation to Mr S. Attariwala Singh, of Enfield
Language Centre and Ambrose Flemming School, for reading the
manuscript and making helpful suggestions.

Illustrated by Gary Long.

Cover photograph by courtesy of Ann and Bury Peerless.

Contents

Introduction

Birthdays are very special days. Your own birthday is special, and you like your family and friends to remember it. In the same way, they like you to remember theirs!

As birthdays *are* special we like to make them different from other days; a birthday calls for celebration. For this reason we give presents and have parties. These are ways of showing that birthdays are important.

People are not only interested in the birthdays of those they know personally. Television, radio and magazines often report the birthdays of famous people. They know that many will be interested in the birthdays of their favourite actors, pop stars or television personalities.

Some people become so famous and important that their birthdays are remembered long after they are dead. The birthdays of inventors, artists, kings, composers and writers are often remembered in this way. For example, Shakespeare's birthday is celebrated every year, especially in the town of Stratford-upon-Avon, where he was born and where the theatre company named after him produces his plays.

In any religion the person who began it is always held in high regard. The founder's birthday usually holds a special place in the minds and hearts of his followers. For instance, Christians celebrate the birthday of Christ every year at Christmas.

Another great religion of the world where the birthday of the founder is a very special festival is Sikhism. Its followers, the Sikhs, remember their founder every November and give great importance to his birthday celebration.

1

Nanak, Founder of the Sikhs

The man who started the religion we know today as Sikhism was Guru Nanak. The word 'guru' has come to mean 'teacher'. It is a title, not a name. The two parts of the word 'gu' and 'ru' mean 'dark' and 'light'. In India a man is given the title of guru when people begin to feel that, as a result of his teaching, they have been led from the darkness of ignorance to the light of understanding. So for much of his life the founder of Sikhism was simply known by his name of Nanak. The title came later.

Nanak was born on 15 April 1469 in a village called Talwandi. It is situated in the north-west corner of India, known as the Punjab. The name 'Punjab' means simply 'land of the five rivers'. It is a very rich and fertile area. For thousands of years it was the gateway to India. The overland trade routes from Europe came through the Punjab and travellers brought both goods and ideas to the people who lived there. When Nanak was born, the whole of the Punjab was inside India. Today it is divided in two, half in India, the other half in Pakistan. This division came about in 1947 when, after much bitter fighting between Hindus (who follow the religion of Hinduism) and Muslims (who follow the Islamic reiigion), a new country, Pakistan, was created to provide an Islamic homeland for the Muslims. Almost half a million people died in the conflict as whole families were uprooted from their homes, including many Sikhs.

Hinduism and Islam were the two main religions in India at the time of Nanak's birth. Nanak himself was born into a Hindu family and was brought up in the ways of Hinduism. His father, however, worked for the owner or landlord of the village. This man was a Muslim. It was a time when the Muslims were in control of much of India even though they were fewer in numbers. Nanak knew this landlord well and as he grew up he learned a lot about both religions. He could see that there was good and bad in each.

As Nanak grew up he thought deeply about religion. The day approached when he could become a full Hindu. On this day he would go through the sacred-thread ceremony — a symbol to show not only that he was a man and a full member of the Hindu religion but also that he was a high-caste Hindu.

All Hindus were divided into strict social classes, or 'castes'. The first caste, Brahmins, belonged to the priestly order and were held to be the closest to God. The lowest order, the 'outcastes', were despised by the rest of society and led very hard lives.

Nanak, although he was still very young, refused to go through the sacred-thread ceremony. Also, he did not believe in the caste system. He thought that Muslims were right to think that everyone was equal in the sight of God. But there were things the Muslims believed that he thought were wrong, such as always turning towards Mecca to pray. It seemed to Nanak that God was everywhere. He did not want to become a Muslim any more than he wanted to be a proper Hindu.

Some time later, while he was still a young man, something happened which was to change Nanak's life. Hindus always wash carefully before praying and Nanak still did this. One day he went down to the river to wash as usual but he did not come back. He was missing for three days. His family and friends began to think he was dead.

After three days, however, he reappeared. He told his friends that while away he had come to realize a marvellous and very simple truth. God was neither a Hindu nor a Muslim. He was just simply God. Nanak told his friends that from that day he was going to follow wherever God would lead him. He would leave behind the religions of both Hindus and Muslims for ever.

The rest of Nanak's life was spent in travelling, teaching everyone he met that they should follow the One God. He won many converts. Nanak's teaching seemed more true to them than that of both the Hindu and the Muslim teachers. These converts became the first Sikhs.

For a long time they met only in small groups, but eventually they came together through the teachings and guidance of Nanak. They gave him the title of guru.

When Nanak died the Sikhs found other gurus to take his place. But because their numbers were small they were easily persecuted by both Hindus and Muslims. Altogether nine gurus followed on from Nanak and it was the last of these who organized the Sikhs into one great brotherhood.

Guru Nanak (from an early Sikh painting)

2

The Roots of Nanak's Religion

The Khalsa

Between 1675 and 1708 the Punjab was torn by war. The Muslim emperor of Afghanistan tried again and again to conquer the Punjab. He also wanted to stamp out the Sikhs, who seemed to be against his own religion.

At this time the last guru, Guru Gobind Singh, called many Sikhs together. He told them that they must be prepared to fight for their religion. He asked if any man would die for his beliefs. One man stepped forward and Guru Gobind Singh took him behind a screen. When the Guru returned he was alone and he carried a sword dripping with blood. He asked again if others would die for their religion. Many of the Sikhs were too afraid but four more men stepped forward. The Guru took each one in turn behind the screen. The Sikhs must have been very afraid, but when the Guru moved back the screen the five men appeared alive, and the bodies of five goats lay on the ground.

The Guru praised the five for their bravey. He then told them that they would be the first members of a brotherhood, or Khalsa, to which all Sikhs would belong. The task of the Khalsa would be to defend Sikhism in order that it might grow.

To show that they belonged to the Khalsa all Sikhs were given new titles. The men would be known as 'Singh', which means 'lion'. The women would be known as 'Kaur', which

11

Guru Gobind Singh

means 'princess'. The Guru also told the Sikhs to wear five symbols to show that they were part of the Khalsa or brotherhood of Sikhism.

The five symbols of Sikhism

The five symbols of Sikhism are usually called the Five K's. This is because the names of the symbols all begin with the letter K. Wherever Sikhs go they can be recognized immediately by the symbols they wear.

The first K is *kesh*. Sikhs never cut their hair or beards. This shows that they believe that no one has the right to interfere with nature. Only God can bring changes into his own natural

A Sikh buying the Five K's from a stall

world. It is obvious that very long hair can soon become untidy and be a nuisance at work. For this reason Sikhs must carry a comb or *kanga*, so that they can keep their hair tidy. Men also make sure that they keep their hair clean by covering it with a turban. This is made from a long strip of cloth which is wound round and round the head. Although the turban is not one of the Five K's, it is probably the thing that most helps people to recognize Sikhs.

As we have seen, Sikhs are willing to fight for their religion and the next two K's show this. In the past men were expected to wear white shorts so that they could fight easily. These are known as *kachs* and are still a common sight in India. However, many Sikhs live in other parts of the world today. Sikhs in Britain find it uncomfortable to wear shorts in our cooler climate and so they usually wear them under trousers.

A more obvious symbol is the *kirpan*, which is a long single-edged sword. In everyday life this is usually

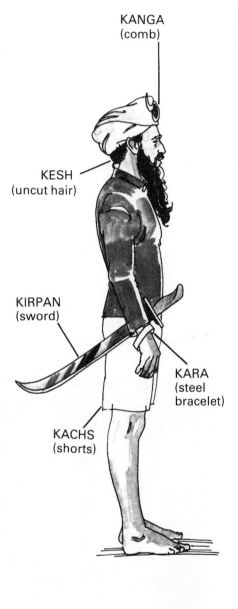

KANGA (comb)

KESH (uncut hair)

KIRPAN (sword)

KARA (steel bracelet)

KACHS (shorts)

The Five K's

seen as a sword-shaped brooch. This brooch is often pinned to the turban. However, on special occasions, such as the celebration of Guru Nanak's birthday, real swords are carried.

The last K is a steel bangle called a *kara* which is worn on the right wrist. It shows that all Sikhs are united in brotherhood. It also shows that Sikhs believe that God is eternal, with no beginning and no end.

All of these symbols must be worn by Sikhs at all times. They are especially important when Sikhs join in religious celebrations. No Sikh would celebrate Guru Nanak's birthday without wearing them.

The Guru Granth Sahib

Many religions have a holy book. For Christians it is the Bible, for Muslims it is the Qur'an. The holy book of the Sikhs is called the Guru Granth Sahib. Many people just call it the Granth.

Just before he died Guru Gobind Singh told Sikhs that they would never have a human guru or teacher again. Instead the book of Sikh scriptures would be the teacher and guide for all Sikhs.

The Granth being read at a Sikh wedding

The Sikhs respect the Granth very deeply and all Sikh families try to have a copy in their home. It is placed in a special upstairs room where the family can study it quietly. The book is always raised on a stand so that it is in a higher position than the members of the family. This shows the deep respect the Sikhs have for the Guru Granth Sahib.

In any Sikh festival the Guru Granth Sahib plays a very important part. This is especially true when Guru Nanak's birthday is celebrated.

3

Celebrating Nanak's Birthday

Some Sikh festivals occur in special places. These may be where Nanak taught or where some important incident took place. There are many sites which are holy to the Sikhs, especially in and around the town of Amritsar, which is the central and sacred city of the Sikh faith.

There are other festivals, called 'universal festivals' by the Sikhs, which can be celebrated anywhere. The celebration of Guru Nanak's birthday is one of these universal festivals.

As we have seen, Guru Nanak was born in April, yet his birthday is celebrated in November each year. The reason for this is probably linked with the Hindu festival Divali,* which takes place in November when the scorching heat of the Indian summer gives way to cooler weather.

The main symbol of Divali is light, and the celebration of light overcoming darkness. It is perhaps the oldest and most popular of all Hindu festivals and almost everyone takes part. It seems likely that the Sikhs also saw November as a good time in which to celebrate the birthday of their founder and guru who *enlightened* them in the ways of God.

Preparing for Guru Nanak's birthday

Such an important festival has to be prepared for very carefully

*See the book *Divali* in this series.

indeed. These preparations are extremely important and form part of the festival itself.

The meeting-place for any Sikh community is the gurdwara, which means 'the house of the guru'. The guru today, of course, is the great guru, the holy book, Guru Granth Sahib. A gurdwara must be big enough for all the community to get inside and, in the Punjab, some of them are very large indeed, standing out in a village just like some large parish churches in Britain. It is in the gurdwara that the celebration of Guru Nanak's birthday begins.

The men make sure that they are wearing the five symbols of Sikhism. When they go into the gurdwara they first take off their shoes. All heads must be covered, however, and anyone who does not have a turban has to find some covering — a clean handkerchief will do.

The women wear traditional Punjabi dress. This is often a beautiful sari or a tunic over light trousers. Their heads are covered with chiffon scarves. Often the women find ornamental ways of wearing some, if not all, of the five symbols.

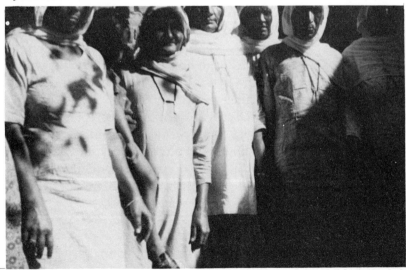

Sikh women with Five K's necklaces

Two days before the birthday proper the ceremonial reading of the Guru Granth Sahib begins. Readers take it in turns to recite or chant aloud the whole book from beginning to end. In Sikhism there are no castes or classes of people and women and men are completely equal. The sacred task of reading the Guru Granth Sahib is done by both.

Once begun the reading continues day and night. Those in the congregation stay for as much of the reading as they can but of course, at some point, most have to leave to go to work, make meals, look after children or relatives. Each person will stay for as long as possible and will return as soon as they can. This is especially true towards the end of the two days. All Sikhs like to attend the final hours and, as the gurdwara begins to fill up, the excitement of a festive occasion increases.

The gurdwara is unusual as a place of worship in that it always has a kitchen. Hospitality is a vitally important thing to Sikhs. No visitor must ever go hungry and eating together is a strong tie of brotherhood. Because of this anyone who comes to the gurdwara can stay as long as he or she wishes.

During the reading of the Guru Granth Sahib this kitchen is used to prepare a ceremonial meal for the festival. This is called karah parshad. It is made from flour, butter, sugar and water, heated together and stirred, often with a sword or kirpan.

The karah parshad is taken to the people who have come to hear the reading of the Granth. The food is taken from only one bowl and each person takes a small amount with the fingers. This token sharing of a meal from the same dish is a symbol that all Sikhs are united in one great brotherhood.

All this means that there must be several people present day and night through the two days. The reading must not stop and there must be others in attendance to meet the readers' needs for food and drink. The sense of being together, of community, gets stronger and stronger as Guru Nanak's birthday comes closer.

Guru Nanak's birthday arrives
At the end of the forty-eight-hour reading of the Guru Granth

A Sikh holding the kirpan

Sahib the serious and solemn preparation for the festival is over. The actual day of Guru Nanak's birthday has arrived. The people can now simply enjoy a cheerful celebration.

A procession begins. The holy book — the Guru Granth Sahib — is to be paraded through the streets. Because it is the most sacred object to the Sikhs the book is treated all the time as if it were a king. In the gurdwara, or in the home, it sits on silk cushions on a raised seat or throne. Often there is a canopy overhead. When it is taken in procession it is carried aloft and accompanied by a guard of honour.

First a wooden float or platform is carefully covered with a richly embroidered cloth. The Guru Granth Sahib is then carefully moved from its place in the gurdwara. It is placed on the float and then Sikh men and women decorate it with the colourful petals of sweet-smelling flowers. The float is then carried out into the streets, often being held up in the air above the heads of the bearers.

The float is followed by five men who form a guard. These five men represent the first five members of the Khalsa who were prepared to die for the brotherhood. Each member of the bodyguard carries a finely worked and richly decorated kirpan.

Procession of the Granth

The rest of the congregation form a carnival-like procession which follows the float through the streets of the town. The mood is now very different from the quiet, serious meeting in the gurdwara. The Sikhs show their joy by singing hymns and chanting prayers. Many of them scatter flower petals as they go through the streets.

From time to time the whole procession stops — usually at a crossroads. Here guest speakers read to the people. Some may read serious passages from the Guru Granth Sahib. Others will tell stories of some of the wonderful exploits of Guru Nanak. When the speaker has finished the whole crowd shouts, 'waheguru', which means 'wonderful guru', a name given to God. This is a way of praising the One God whom Nanak taught about.

At the end of the day the Sikhs replace the Guru Granth Sahib on its throne in the gurdwara. Then all the people who have taken part in the celebrations return to their homes. There is a real sense of belonging to one great family.

The festival in Amritsar
Guru Nanak's birthday, as we have seen, is a universal festival. The description given above is a very general one and there are variations in different places.

Wherever they may be in the world on Guru Nanak's birthday almost all Sikhs will give some thought to the celebrations in the city of Amritsar. Amritsar means 'the place of nectar or honey'. It is the centre of the Sikh brotherhood and the Sikh religion. It is there that the Golden Temple stands, a place which is sacred to all Sikhs. Many have died defending it from invasion.

The walls of the temple are covered with sheets of beaten gold which shine brightly in the sun. It stands in the middle of a huge pool and can be reached only by a narrow pontoon, or 'floating bridge'. The gateway to the pontoon is also made of beaten gold.

On Guru Nanak's birthday the temple and its surrounds are full. Around the edges of the sacred pool hundreds of small

The Golden Temple at Amritsar

ghee lamps flicker inside earthenware saucers (ghee is a type of oil made from the butter of Indian buffalo milk). For much of the time people stand around talking and meeting friends. It is a very relaxed occasion but in the middle of it all small ceremonies are being performed throughout the day.

As they enter the temple area around the pool most Sikhs light a candle and place it on one of the many stands. These add to all the flickering lights at the edge of the pool (similar lights are placed out in the streets in many Indian towns at this time by Hindus celebrating the festival of Divali). As darkness falls the thousands of candle flames are reflected in the water and give enough light to reflect the Golden Temple as well. It is a magnificent sight.

While this is happening all round the pool there is a constant procession out along the pontoon into the temple itself. There the reading of the Guru Granth Sahib continues. The slow, constant procession goes through the temple, round and back along the pontoon. There is just room on the pontoon for two files of people to pass.

Because it is a special day — perhaps the most special day in the year for Sikhs — every effort has been made to decorate the temple even more richly. As darkness falls it can be seen that the temple and the pontoon gateway are draped with coloured lights which add their reflections to the brightness of the pool.

The festival in Britain

Many Sikhs now live and work in Britain, where they also celebrate Guru Nanak's birthday. In November each year they meet in their own gurdwaras although, with their numbers being fairly small, they do not always have a procession through the streets.

As in other parts of the world, Sikhs in Britain carry out the continuous reading of the Guru Granth Sahib at this time. But afterwards they will probably go to their homes for a normal birthday party celebration together. We must remember, too, that even if there were enough Sikhs in one place for the

Gurdwaras in Britain are often in ordinary houses, like this one in Exeter

Inside the Gurdwara – Exeter

normal procession the weather in Britain in November might not always make it practicable.

In 1969, though, British Sikhs decided they must make a special attempt to celebrate this birthday properly whatever the difficulties. That was because that year was the 500th anniversary of the birth of Nanak.

Sikhs from all over Britain organized a procession through the streets of London. The Guru Granth Sahib was carried aloft and given pride of place at the head of the column. It was all done exactly as it happens in India only on this occasion groups of Sikhs set out from different parts of London and met up at the Royal Albert Hall, which had been hired especially for the occasion. British gurdwaras are small and Indian ones are sometimes very large but on this day the largest Sikh meeting-place in the world was in London.

Inside the Hall the normal activities went on. Hymns were sung, stories of Nanak were told and parts of the Guru Granth Sahib were read. For those Sikhs who felt cut off from their fellow Sikhs in India it was a very moving occasion. It drew everybody together as one family, a great brotherhood of men, women and children held together by the teaching and the inspiration of a man who walked the plains of the Punjab five centuries ago.

4

The Meaning

A great many festivals celebrate just one aspect of a religion, like the Christian Easter, which is about the Resurrection; the Jewish Passover, which tells of the freeing of the Jews from captivity; or the Hindu Divali, which celebrates the victory of light over darkness in the story of Rama and Sita (there are books on all these festivals in this series).

Guru Nanak's birthday is different. It does not emphasize his birth or childhood. This celebration is about everything that Nanak said and did, and about what it means to be a Sikh. It is as if on this day Sikhs throughout the world were saying together, 'We are Sikhs — and we are proud of it'.

The reading of the Guru Granth Sahib from beginning to end emphasizes that this festival is about all the teaching which Nanak gave and which the other gurus continued. Sikhism is a very broad and tolerant religion. We have seen how Nanak came to believe that other religions were too narrow and seemed to limit the presence of God. Nanak's teaching emphasized a quiet and hardworking type of life with great stress on honesty and seeking after goodness.

Above all Sikhism is about belonging together, of helping one another. Throughout their history Sikhs have often been persecuted because they did not belong to either Islam or Hinduism. The sense of brotherhood is very strong and the festival celebrations we have been describing involve the whole community. It is this sense of togetherness or fellowship

which is made strong again every year as the followers of
Nanak and his teaching come together to celebrate his
birthday.

THINGS TO DO

1 Say or write down why you think birthdays are important. Does it matter how they are celebrated? Is the age of the person always the most important thing?
  Either describe a birthday party you have been to **or** say what is particularly special about (a) An eighteenth birthday (b) The Queen's birthday (c) Shakespeare's birthday.
2 Copy out the map of India and Pakistan showing where the Punjab is. Try and give some reasons why its position has affected what happened there.
3 Write the story of the beginning of the Khalsa brotherhood as if you were there as one of the Sikhs taking part. Describe your own thoughts and fears along with what was happening to everyone else.
4 Draw a picture of a Sikh man wearing the five symbols of his religion.
5 Describe any object which you regard as sacred? Is there any symbolic way of showing its importance? For example, is it kept high up on a wall, hidden away except for special occasions, or decorated?
6 Organize a 'read in', so that a group of people read through a book or a play without stopping.
7 Try to think of several reasons why eating a meal together has long been regarded as a sign of close friendship. How many religions can you think of which have special meals as part of their worship or festival celebrations?

8 Try to arrange a visit to a local gurdwara by contacting the President. Notice in particular all the symbols of greatness surrounding the Guru Granth Sahib. Make sure that you find out beforehand if there are special things you must wear and do everything necessary to show respect.

9 'It does not matter what you think about God; it is what you think about other people which is important.'
'People only feel they belong together when they all feel they belong to the same God.'
Discuss these two statements.

10 If you have already done some work on Islam and Hinduism discuss why it is that you think Sikhs want to be different from both.

MATERIAL FOR TEACHERS

Useful addresses

The Sikh Cultural Society
17 Abbotshill Road
Catford
London SE6 1SQ

The Sikh Missionary Society
20 Peacock Street
Gravesend
Kent

Education Department
Commission for Racial
  Equality
10-12 Allington Street
London SW1 5EH

Shap Working Party
7 Alderbrook Road
Solihull
West Midlands B91 1NH

(Enclose stamped addressed envelope when writing to the above.)

Books to read about the Sikhs

Butler, B. G. *Life Among Sikhs.* Edward Arnold.
Farncombe, A. *Our Sikh Friends.* National Christian Education Council.
Lyle, S. *Pavan is a Sikh.* A. & C. Black, 1977.
Owen Cole, W. *A Sikh Family in Britain.* The Religious Education Press, 1978.
———————. *Thinking About Sikhism.* Lutterworth.
Sambhi, P. S. *Understanding Your Sikh Neighbours.* Lutterworth.

Workcards

Rankin, John. *Looking at Festivals.* Lutterworth.

Assembly books on festivals

Green, Victor. *Festivals and Saints Days.* Blandford.
Purton, Rowland. *Festivals and Celebrations.* Blackwell, 1979.
Smith, Harry. *Assemblies.* Heinemann, 1981.